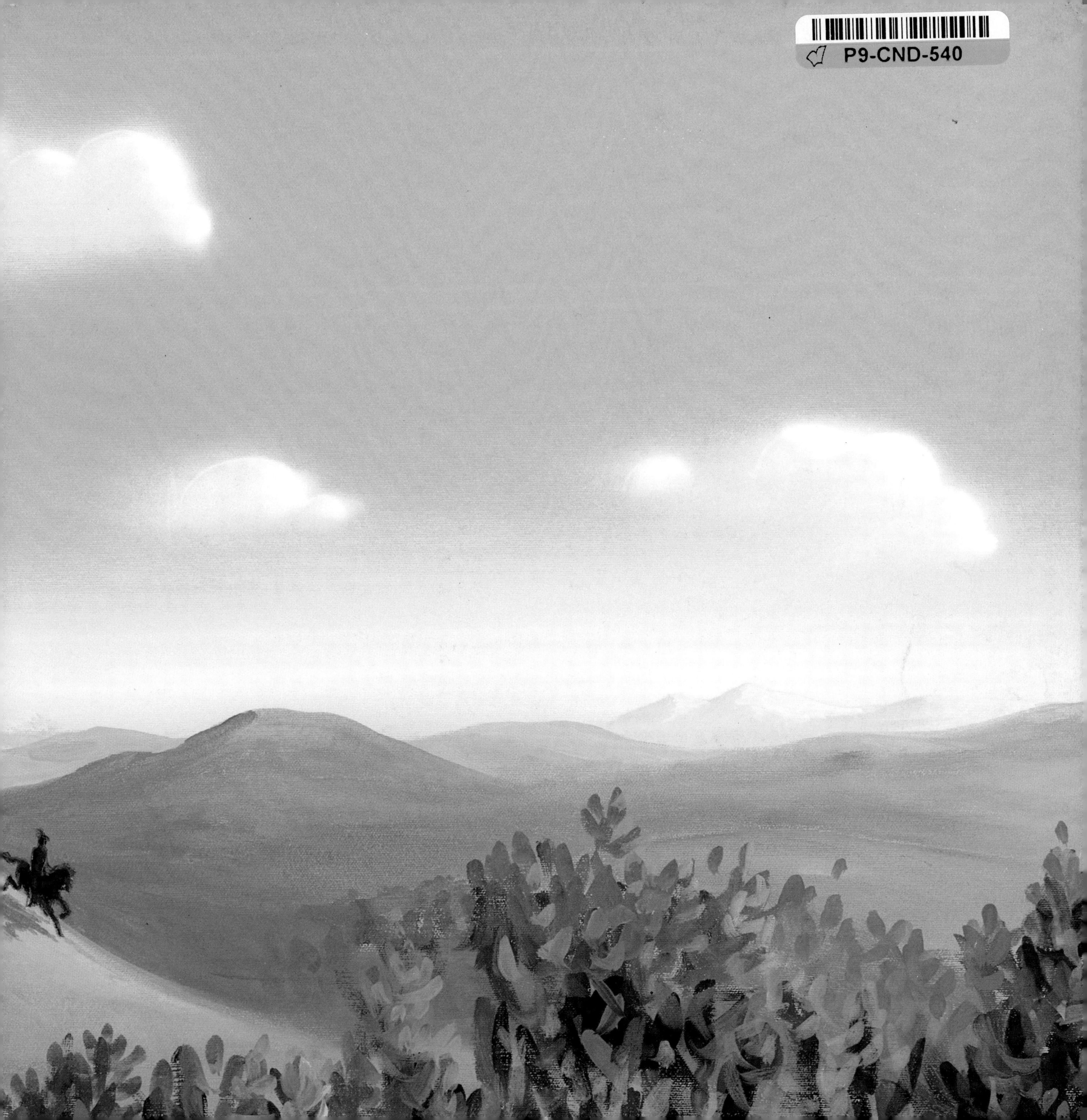

ONCE UPON A TIME

CAN YOU SEE WHAT I SEE?
ONCE UPON A TIME

by Walter Wick

SCHOLASTIC INC.

New York   Toronto   London   Auckland   Mexico City   Sydney

New Delhi   Hong Kong   Buenos Aires

Published by Scholastic Inc.

SCHOLASTIC, CARTWHEEL BOOKS, and

associated logos are trademarks and/or

registered trademarks of Scholastic Inc.

ISBN: 0-439-61777-4

10 9 8 7 6 5 4 3 2 1   06 07 08 09 10/0

Printed in Mexico 49

First printing, September 2006

Book Design by Walter Wick and David Saylor

FOR MELANIE & LOUISE WORD

Library of Congress Cataloging-in-Publication Data

Wick, Walter.

Can you see what I see? Once upon a time : picture puzzles to search

and solve / by Walter Wick.   p. cm.

ISBN 0-439-61777-4

1. Picture puzzles—Juvenile literature. 2. Fairy tales. I. Title.

GV1507.P47W5134 2006

793.73--dc22   2006005853

CONTENTS

THREE LITTLE PIGS   11

LITTLE RED RIDING HOOD   12

HANSEL & GRETEL   15

BEAUTY & THE BEAST   16

GOLDILOCKS   19

SLEEPING BEAUTY   20

THE LITTLE MERMAID   23

STEADFAST TIN SOLDIER   24

PUSS IN BOOTS   27

RUMPELSTILTSKIN   28

CINDERELLA   31

EVER AFTER   32

ABOUT THIS BOOK   34

ABOUT THE AUTHOR   35

Can you see
what I see?
A hammer, a hatchet,
a watering can,
a sewing needle,
a frying pan,
a bunny, 5 birds,
2 boots, a barn,
6 ears of corn,
a red ball of yarn,
a saw, 2 shovels,
a windup mouse,
a snug little pig
in his sturdy brick
house!

Can you see
what I see?
A comb, 2 slippers,
3 forks, a spoon,
a clothespin, a cat,
a matchstick, a moon,
a thimble, a thumbtack,
a horse and rider,
a rolling pin,
a jug for cider,
a fish, 2 frogs,
a girl in red,
and a wicked wolf
in Grandma's bed!

Can you see
what I see?
A wolf that howls,
a bear that's sweet,
a broom, a bat,
2 worms to eat,
an owl, an acorn,
an ax, a nail,
a deer, a dove,
a shovel, a snail,
a red raspberry,
a rolling pin,
a witch who beckons,
"Come in, come in!"

Can you see
what I see?
A pelican,
3 ships, a whale,
a lizard with
a curly tail,
a frog, a turtle,
a kangaroo,
an elephant,
4 monkeys, too,
a crown adorned
with good luck charms,
and Beast at peace
in Beauty's arms.

Can you see
what I see?
A turtle, 3 fish,
2 squirrels, a bunny,
an acorn cap,
a pot for honey,
a bear paw print,
a button, a bat,
a dragonfly,
a fisherman's hat,
a kettle for cooking,
a spool for thread,
and long golden locks
in a little bear's bed!

Can you see
what I see?
A dragon's shadow,
a spinning wheel,
a golden fan,
a pink high heel,
seven gold goblets,
seven-league boots,
a wicked fairy
of twisted roots,
a dashing prince
on a hill so steep,
a lovely princess
in a deep, deep sleep!

Can you see
what I see?
A hammerhead shark,
a scissor-tailed fish,
a ship in a bottle,
a blue-and-white dish,
7 sea horses,
a lobster, an eel,
a rusty old cannon,
a rod and reel,
11 starfish,
an anchor, a comb,
and the shell-topped castle
a mermaid calls home!

Can you see
what I see?
A clock at midnight,
a goblin, a rat,
a jack-in-the-box,
a goose in a hat,
a bell, 10 drummers,
a donkey, 2 dogs,
a big bad wolf,
5 musical frogs,
a steadfast soldier,
standing so smart,
and a lovely dancer
who's stolen his heart.

Can you see
what I see?
A fox, 4 rabbits,
a pinecone, a pear,
a torch, a trumpet,
an archer, a bear,
7 black birds,
a windmill, a well,
a dragon, a deer,
a basket, a bell,
the marquis's carriage,
a white-plumed hat,
an ogre's frown,
and one clever cat!

Can you see
what I see?
A unicorn,
a cradle, a crown,
a golden sun
that's upside down,
7 spiders,
a fly, a bee,
an elephant,
a lock, a key,
a wheel to spin,
a fan to fold,
and RUMPELSTILTSKIN,
revealed in gold!

Can you see
what I see?
A broken heart,
a knight, a moon,
an instrument
that plays a tune,
a pumpkin coach,
an owl, a hare,
a butterfly,
a teddy bear,
a rat in a hat,
a prince in blue,
and Cinderella's
slipper, too!

Can you see
what I see?
A red brick oven,
a goblin, 4 bears,
5 fish, a mermaid,
a prince on the stairs,
2 witches, 2 wolves,
a dragon, 3 dogs,
a gingerbread house,
an acorn, 2 frogs,
a mouse that's worried,
a pig that's mending—
now all together
for a happy ending!

For this search-and-find adaptation of eleven classic tales, I chose a dramatic moment from each story and created a sketch that highlighted characters and plot elements. Using a mountain of raw materials, including paper, paint, plastic, clay, fabric, wood, and toys, I worked with a dedicated team of staff members and artists who transformed my two-dimensional designs into three-dimensional sets. Using a camera, lights, and some digital sleight of hand, I transformed the sets back to two dimensions.

While arranging each set, I thought about words and phrases that would evoke ideas from the story, and then finalized the rhyme just before I shot the photograph. The entire process took six months.

Acknowledgments: It's been my great privilege to work with the dedicated team of staff members and freelance artists who made this book possible. I'm deeply grateful. I'd like to thank my longtime studio manager, Dan Helt, who supervised operations in the workshop, built models, rigged sets, and provided expert computer, camera, and postproduction support. I'd like to thank prop manager Kim Wildey for patiently keeping track of thousands of props, for providing invaluable assistance on set, and for her versatile artistic talents. A very special thanks to the freelance artists: to Randy Gilman, who made the castles for "Sleeping Beauty" and "Steadfast Tin Soldier" and transformed polyurethane foam into trees, landscapes, log cabins, furniture, stone walls, fireplaces, rooftops, a spinning wheel, and numerous other details for "Hansel and Gretel," "Three Little Pigs," "Little Red Riding Hood," "Goldilocks," "Puss in Boots," "Rumpelstiltskin," and "Beauty and the Beast"; to Michael Lokensgaard, who made the castles for "Little Mermaid" and "Cinderella," painted the backdrop for "Sleeping Beauty," and manipulated polymers and paint to create many props and most of the principal characters for the book, including the pigs in "Three Little Pigs," the wolf in "Little Red Riding Hood," the cat, mouse, and lion in "Puss in Boots," and the working duck fountains in "Beauty and the Beast"; to Lynne Steincamp, who made costumes, wigs, and bedding for "Sleeping Beauty," "Goldilocks," "Beauty and the Beast," "Little Red Riding Hood," and "Puss in Boots"; and to Michael Galvin for building and sculpting many details in sets for "Goldilocks," "Puss in Boots," "Rumpelstiltskin," "Steadfast Tin Soldier," and "Beauty and the Beast." Thanks to Eric Zafaran and Susan Hood for providing historical references; to Sharique Ansari of Digicon Imaging Inc. for his superb color separations; and finally, a heartfelt thanks to my wife, Linda, for her profound artistic wisdom and unfailing support.

I'd like to thank Grace Maccarone and Ken Geist for encouraging me to venture into storyland; and to David Saylor, Stephen Hughes, and Scott Myles for their excellent contributions to the book design. —Walter Wick

All sets were designed, arranged, photographed, and digitally retouched by the author. Spot illustrations were arranged by Randy Gilman and photographed by Dan Helt. The painting that appears on the endpapers and as the backdrop of "Sleeping Beauty" is by Michael Lokensgaard.

Walter Wick is the photographer of the I Spy series of books, with more than twenty-nine million copies in print. He is author and photographer of *A Drop of Water: A Book of Science and Wonder*, which won the Boston Globe/Horn Book Award for Nonfiction, was named a Notable Children's Book by the American Library Association, and was selected as an Orbis Pictus Honor Book and a CBC/NSTA Outstanding Science Trade Book for Children. *Walter Wick's Optical Tricks*, a book of photographic illusions, was named a Best Illustrated Children's Book by the *New York Times Book Review*, was recognized as a Notable Children's Book by the American Library Association, and received many awards, including a Platinum Award from the Oppenheim Toy Portfolio, a Young Readers Award from *Scientific American*, a *Bulletin* Blue Ribbon, and a Parents' Choice Silver Honor. *Can You See What I See?*, published in 2003, appeared on the *New York Times* Bestseller List for twenty-two weeks. His most recent books in the Can You See What I See? series are *Dream Machine*, *Cool Collections*, and *The Night Before Christmas*. Mr. Wick has invented photographic games for *GAMES* magazine and photographed covers for books and magazines, including *Newsweek, Discover*, and *Psychology Today*. A graduate of Paier College of Art, Mr. Wick lives in Connecticut with his wife, Linda.

More information about this book and other books by Walter Wick is available at www.walterwick.com.